I0080076

liminal woman

Leticia Mooney

Copyright © 2023 by Leticia Mooney.
All rights reserved.
No part of this publication may be reproduced, distributed, or transmitted in
any form or by any means, including photocopying, recording, or other
electronic or mechanical methods, without the prior written permission of the
publisher, except as permitted by copyright law. For permission requests,
contact the author direct via her website at https://leticiamooney.com.
The author asserts ownership of all moral rights.
Book Cover by Leticia Mooney.
First edition, 1 Setptember 2023.

For Beren. You're more of a gift than you can possibly imagine.

Acknowledgements

Stepping into my life as an artist would not be possible without the following:

My infant son, Beren, whose gift of time given to me during naps has been a real blessing. Thanks to you, and the existence of pen and paper, my art has found new ways into the world.

To Troy, the beautiful man I married, whose unfailing belief and exhortations to 'just do, don't think!': You have been truly enabling.

Thanks to my mum Therese and my mum-in-law Uta, artists both; the former has always believed in me, and the latter introduced me to Julia Cameron's amazing program, *The Artist's Way*.

Thanks to the other writers in my life, especially Tobias Crush and Scott Mooney, whose vulnerability, enthusiasm and support have done more for my art than anything else.

And for planting the seeds of possibility, my gratitude goes to fellow Australian author Ly de Angeles, whose no-bullshit attitude exhorted me to just 'get dirty and write'.

… No contents page?

No, none. I have chosen to eliminate a contents page because poetry isn't linear and the titles are largely irrelevant unless you've already read the poems. Dip in and out at your leisure in any order. Use this page for notes instead, if you wish.
Xx Leticia

Freedom To

Hidden in the darkened depths
Among he debris of industrial life
Is a cellar, devoid of egress.

It is buried up to its eyeballs.
The one shaft of light filtering into its cold and unwelcome
hovel
Is high-up, cold, and barred.

This cellar was built one brick at a time;
Bricks gathered from the walling waste of a quiet,
Sneaky demolition.

For every brick cemented into the tiny prison,
Ten fell from the outer face.
More fell from inner walls, unseen.

Brick by brick the cellar was built,
Doorless and starless and unforgiving,
Around a frightened girl who was
Barely walking.

She climbed once, twice, and fell so hard that her skin broke,
Her spirit crumbled,
And she sat.

The walls grew, piece by piece
Until they were so tall
She could barely see the top.
The barred window set high and narrow, was not designed for
hope.

The outer bricks continued to fall,
And as the girl howled in fear and panic and horror

The final piece fell into place and the
Cement rain muffled her cries
In a ghastly curtain of soundproofing by force.

Years passed.

As she grew, she lost her voice for the screaming;
Forgot how to walk;
Became limp with atrophy.

She lost her nails and her fingertips in her attempts to escape,
The inner walls coated in her body's rust,
Her soul splattered and scratched,
Dripped and torn
Across the crude brickwork in the darkness and the cold,
Waiting for that time,
Some unknown, magickal, time
In which she would again
Find herself in the light;
Not knowing that she would be blinded and maimed,
Destroyed and afraid,
Shattered into a jigsaw of a million pieces,
Not knowing that the putting-together could be as painful as the
Tearing apart.

Time is a tape that comes off the reel
Never to be replaced
Or caught up.

Still she waited, deathless and suspended;
Unaware that in her suspense and emotion
She created
Ripples that became the weather,
The structures surrounding her,
The birdsong and the tides,
The very air thick with painful regret.

Until a mighty earthquake began to
Rattle the Earth under where she sat.
It increased her terror, yet her
Wailing caused the grinding gears of
The planet's hidden mechanism
To gain velocity,
Protesting against the aged, rusted
Metals that howled with every movement.
Increasing each judder to a mighty collision that
Eventually caused the walls to crack,
To shift,
To admit light.

Light seared through the gaps in shafts of brilliance,
Making dust motes sparkle;
Passing a cool, fresh breeze that
Bathed the girl in the refreshing stream
Of wonder.

The gaps, large enough for fingers;
The damage, intense enough to loosen bricks.

Knowing not the extent of her binds
Nor the infinite possibility awaiting her,
The girl very, very gently began to break free.

The fallen bricks surrounding her cold
Cave of torture began to dissolve:
Ten for every brick she managed to
Prise loose and cast away;
More dissolved from inner walls unseen
Until she sat,
Unearthed.

Unprotected.

Vulnerable and fragile, in a world

Exciting and unknown,
Forced only to trust this divinity that
Had given her this freedom.

So she picked up a brick shard, and in the
Fallen dust
Began to write.

Turned Inwards

How many acts of
Self-destruction can we take
Before the sunrise?

It's A Social Cancer

I see the politicisation of events
In a society that makes women men
And convinces them it's freedom.

Yet how many get cancer
From putting their needs last?
That soft, nurturing breast tissue
Clogged with lumps
As if it's some modern chemical affliction,
Making me scream it IS dopamine -
But it's your addiction to a
Success created by and for men
Designed to destroy the
Liminal female.

Screaming, because it happened to me too.

But I saw it,
I felt it,
I danced with it.

I became.

The fire of motherhood
Burned away the last lies,
And in its place
Only truth remained.

Society's Perpetual Malady

Sing me a song of being led astray,
Entranced by possibility.
Sparkling like a perpetual summer's day;
That place of ownership, self-owned left
Blurs into others with strength
Of character, who is who is me is you, er, right?

Conditioned in a family culture,
Enticed by exploration in worlds
New and fresh, your right-angle turn seems to make a
Whole lot of sense
Until you lose who you are and make
Decisions that are We not Me, or You, instead.

Losing your grip on your dreams, perhaps,
Scattering to the winds all of your maps,
Then falling to mediocre not-chance.

The maiden is futile, she drifts on the breeze.
Light, young and carefree,
She handles with ease
Each objection that surfaces, comments that bite;
She waves it away
With strength and with might
Until… it no longer works.

What happens when
That maiden stays maiden?
She never listens to broody old hens
Who warn her of nature, of time, of grief.

With platitudes and ire poured over her head
She will suffer, alone, hidden away, build a reef

That becomes so much cancer
Instead of allowing life to fulfil her.

The maiden is teen and is 20s, that's all;
Somehow we've enabled a maiden perpetually
Alive, instead of accepting her wizened footfall
Down the hall into motherhood
Where, fearfully stepping,
Maidens are shed
Of their finery, in preference to a deep initiation
That shreds what's known and
Rebuilds life from station to station.

In which time becomes known for
Her feminine cycles;
Of things done, always done, done yet again.
It's a chore before mother, and joyful not ideal.

Tasks! Suddenly plants grow.
Fed with love and attention
Because mamas are people who, in nurturing, just know
When and how and why not to let slide…

But the maiden is selfish—
Strange that she can hide
Her lights in some other, foreign person's way,
Not realising she is
In charge of her day.

So many influences cause her to coast
Along carefree until she's
Thirty and alone;
Then time brings to bear all of the sadness
Welling in pools in her cave,
Feeling the wasted time.

Descent into madness
Ensues. The old cat lady
Simply never grew.

Perpetual maiden:
Society's malady.

Inconvenient Truth

The program is strong;
You'll fight it until you don't.
Mirror enemy.

Saboteur

At the moment in which
Participation is
Seen, known heartbreakingly
As the imprisoning
Force, that willing teaming-
Up with narcissistic
Abuse, freedom screams in rage.

You collaborated
In good faith, dreaming that
This was co-creation
When it was really
Co-destruction. Merging,
And in merging losing
Access to the Muse's well.

For in that merger
You lost half of yourself;
Become just one half
Of the artist you were.
Destined to incomplete,
To stumble and to fail:
Shadowed without realising.

But the dawning sight sees
All. Recovering from
The blindness, feel body-
Rage, waves of pure anger
Engulfing your cells and
Rallying impotently
Against enemies long gone.

In its wake, cankerous
Sores from your soul sick-

Ness emerging on skin
From inside to outside.
First steps in healing this
Sabotage's leprosy.

Then I Turned 40

Adult life Forty
Business, not babies, please miss,
In absence I cry.

Silence

In the quiet of days
We pass each other
And without menace simply
Not speak.

Three days and three nights
Pass; then a meeting
And a bursting dam
Of excitement
In realising that this flowering

Is perfection.

Nanna

She emerged on high heel
Shoes, black-dressed, young, poise-filled,
Hands clasped, she smiled at me.
'This is a gift,' murmured.
I felt all time dissolve away.

Seeded

It was in that early
Moment of realising that
I was becoming Mother
That all of my powers
Of foresight disappeared,
Only to be replaced by
A mental blindness.
A forcing of Present.

A long, dark tunnel of
Not knowing, not feeling
The future or my
Control.

In its place welled a love
So intense and
So fulfilling and
So ecstatic that
It became, is, and remains,
Timeless.

Belly

From behind: Normal.
From the side: Holy moly!
Buy everything blue.

Dissolving Bridges

The tension between worlds
Stretched, taught, razor-sharp,
Tenuous and fragile.

It helped that the world went crazy.

But the crazymakers all bleated the same, three-word tune:
Employ! Run! Continue!

Surrounded by a cacophony of Same
Billionaire to micro-biz
I reached out and slammed the door.

We'll wait! Clients cried.
Brave move! Some said.

Nobody waited for the return;
Not even those professing undying love.

It granted me peace,
Focus, clarity; a way into
The dark tunnel of Not Knowing,
Forcing a Beginner's Mind to reign
Unbidden.

Once, standing on the opposite bank,
I looked behind me quickly enough
To see the bridge fall and the
Landscape disappear into a strange joy.

Mapless, and without compass or guidance,
I turned to face this new, strange land
Alone.

Darkfalls

Maiden to Mother:
Non-linear, not "awake!"
Burned, screaming, in fire.

Tortuous ending.
Shed skins and self and I AM;
It's not victory.

Trembling, pale flesh, soft.
All weather hits painfully,
Armour not yet grown.

Fitful footfalls took
Stumbling down this darkened path.
No light, no time: Is.

The tunnel is long,
Traversed by heart-light and trust.
Step. Step. Step. Step. Step.

Infinite

Pregnant, you see the
World as it is,
Glorious connectedness.
Regain ancestral knowing
From plant to creature.
Become Queen of the Forest,
Mother to many,
Gifted with the sight and the insight
To understand this realm in
All her magick and horror.

How then do you allow yourself
To forget?
To return from that glade
Of sunlit glory in which all wisdom
Is yours, mine, and ours,
Safe-guarded and kept sacred,
To be used and enjoyed and told in
Tales and verse for the betterment
Of Mankind?

Allow instead that deep connecting
To keep you in step with your
Nature, to enrich you forever
Lest you lose it again, again,
Becoming slave to a world
Whose frogmarch is not
Of this Earth.

Swallow the snake oil

Black, snake-like, oily river,
A grief unknown to women of the age.
Sliding, sticky, residue heavy,
Seen briefly at birth,
Grieving for all the children
You never had,
In a moment of recognition of waste.

All those years
Pretending to be things you're not,
When your true nature is this.

This.

This channel, open portal to the
Creation and emergence of new people,
Magical and godlike,
Through you.

Humans!
By and of you: Love everlasting!

But modernity lies and you eat it,
A soylent green of being.

Grieve.

Grieve for lost time.

This Is The Secret

In the excitement of our wait for you
We prepared a homebirth,
In a pool.

Granted this, our dearest wish,
We thanked our stars and healthiness.
And then one day you turned around,
Our wishes were now upside-down!

We began to do a million things:
Incense and headstands and swimming lanes.
I heard how women just like me
Often have position 'B',
And that no matter what I do
It's baby's choice if it's the sunroof.

Again I faced that wall of fate,
Doing things another's way.

The headstrong youth did real slow
But when finally I did let go

It was perfect.

A Tale Of Two For One

The seed, in growing,
Consumes the soil
In which it grows.

A mother, in becoming,
Devours her soul
In which she'd lived.

Discinarnating
By way of becoming.
Not so much *made*
As *forged* into New.

It's not about pain or
The bloodiest of -ness
But where she goes to:

Before recovering -ness,
Birth is a forge;
Creating not one but Two.

Because Maiden is dying.
Mother born anew,
Time passing shines a light.

Square pegness rules it
A life gone, dead, past.
This new rule is blooming.

An empire is born.
And with it this Mother
Whose life felt forlorn.

In this creation,
Created so much.
Not just this life, this
Precious, this wonder,
But her own new
Coherence, in power,

In thunder.

Embracing the shift
Takes courage, understanding,
And shrift:

To be the change requires
Shedding;
A new gift.

In coherence is Mother:
Reformed, new, whole.
That the maiden couldn't have foreseen,

Much less
Sought to show.

Over The Threshold

Weeks of staring at
This new human, sweetly smell
The season of birth.

Best Thing I Ever Made

Staring: Hours and days
Lost in your magnificence.
Amazed. I made you.

Perfect

Perfection may not exist
But seeing you
Made me realise
Just how close we can get.

Barely An Infant

Your perfect skin and
Your new, wise eyes
Shine into the world
Like beacons of an ancient time.
Infinite love, petals unfurl.

Beren

Boy of mine—
Everlasting love
Real and meaningful.
Evaluating your world;
New, not ignorant.

Red Pill

Lost in oceans of
Eternity
I find the business life
Strange,
Distastefully
Mechanistic.
Plucking flowers:
Beheading them.

Scattered stems fill pathways;
Their shattered reality
Celebrated in a hideous
Theatre of malformed
Lives destroyed, just half-filled.

Thudding realisation
Lands hard; years of lies
Woven into sparkly golden treasure
Gathered close;

One is not forest.

Portal

Nobody explained.
You birth a human being,
Your heart gets new eyes?

Constant Artistry

In the dust-motes of time
Both infinite and perpetual
Co-existing,
Looping
In
f
i
n
i
t
e
l
y
around,
The artist is constant
And maiden versus mother
A simple construct
of
L I N E A R I T Y.
Itself a falseness,
Constructed to stop
The ego from fragmenting
And leaving us
I
N
PIECES
Sad,
That existing Now is so
Damnably difficult—
Until you are looped
In the cyclic time of
Mother,
Of sleep boob change play
Forced into the

~ Stillness ~
Which is what gives rise to
Happy, and
            Sh!
Creativity.

In this way, even
With the artist constant
The maiden is busy
In the romantic sunsets,
Chasing goals and shedding time;
Mothers are mothers
By way of creation and
In the act of giving
Self to mothering
Give rise to the time of the artist.

Creativity rises,
            INSISTS on acknowledgement,
Lest, like the full
Waterfall of a winter's river,
It crashes into consciousness
Destroying reality along the way.

They Need Guides

Losing my sight, and sense
Of my future and goals
Only to exist in
A quiet, blinkered state
Of mind-blindness/deafness
I carried Self; mute, onwards.

Somehow nothing broke down
Except my understanding of
Who I am and how
To relate to others;
Others I know and love,
Strangers now, in this new life.

This was all unforeseen.

The Sisterhood, quiet.
Women, keeping secrets,
In how to navigate
These treacherous waters
Making life hard by absence.

Speak, lest tongues are removed!
Honour, lest you're cut loose!
Open, show them the way!
In you, community
Begins. Let them in.
Show them.

Metamorphosis

Opening a heart-channel
Into the mode of creation allows
A wondrous state to enable
Through the flow of ceaseless time.

It is something hidden, lost, secret,
Known only to women who birth;
The process of change is
Of an immensity
So dire and beautiful
One's eyes are wet.

The moment of shift takes time, it's true.
It's not a speedy thing.
The body will grow inside of you
But you will grow, take wing.

In months of grief and identity shift,
Of fearing potential loss
Your very nature becomes someone else:
A rock grown over with moss.

No matter the method
Of knife or squished passage,
Birthing is not about You.
It's someone else in control of you now.
A moment of breath and life, too.

Just as art is a work, a statement of space,
Which takes over in Zone
To become what it will,
That will is not your Will;
A divine-planned outfill-

Ing of a plan not your own.

Life wants us to think,
Not to feel, not to heart;
Society all gone wrong.
It's why we hate art,
And women destroyed before long.

A sickness has taken over our lives
Where men count as women
And women—begone!
Your sex is invalid, your breasts merely chests
Forget you as sacred: It's wrong.

We're losing the gentle art of the female;
A process of deep transforming
Of people and artwork,
Families hale and hearty,
Lost in fruitless forming
Away from our natures.

Afraid of the fire.

The Woman in conversation with God.
This process, this mystery,
The Goddess made flesh,
Whose Portal,
Whose Earth,
Can't be trod.

Breathing the fire she learns just to flow,
Become who she needs to be,
In order that you can be born; when you know
The time is ripe, you're ready.

Just as art isn't muscle, it's all just water
Gushing down the rock face

Eroding and shaping and being unstill
Changing every facet and face.

Herald Of A Shift

Placeholder gaps
Where poetry should go,
Held open for that time
In which brain and space
Coalesce.
But it didn't.

Energy

An artist needs space:
Mind. Time. Peace, Breathing, feeling.
Luxury is heart.

It's Elastic

Space, like time, will
Contract and expand in
Line with focus and
Clear attention.
       Cascades of flowing energy
       Follow
Form and allowing.
Stare at the clock-face.
"Now" is each number.
Here is space.
Not then.

Sign 'Yes', Here.

When the King Tide eases
The sand is sometimes gone.
Landscapes change,
Debris fills hollows,
Weeds drape rocks,
Calm rhythm returns to the edge space
Where meets NoTime and Man.

Vision extends in clarity,
Feet finding paths beyond the
Regular reptilian pattern,
Discovering a new way of being
In this old place washed anew.

The body adapts, but the mind
Is forever altered in its motion;
Identifying, cataloguing, standing still
In the eye of
A storm who cycles in
The natural state of this
Thing we call time, that we
Somehow see as a ruler
And a rule,
Stepwise, not returning.

Resting now in this place,
Colours become meaningful and
Wildlife becomes part of you, and
Those trees with whom you felt
Kindred while baking this most precious of items
Are sisters—
Felt, majestic, unspoken, sentience
Resonating through all ages.

You might not be draped in
The cloths of royalty
But you are in and of Earth;
Reconnected,
Forever altered,
Existing within a world gone mad with pointless structures
That are now clear,
Obviously superficial,
Even ridiculous.

The breeze cooling your
Decolletage reminds you to
Breathe in this new place, to
Own this new-old skin,
Ancient and vibrant,
Owning every moment of its rhythm,
Forever changed.

Remember to tell that person
In the mirror
That progress means
Not going back.

Woman As Artist

How did we become
So fragmented and lost,
That we forgot that our
Insanely powerful
Ability to
Create is what makes
Women magnifique:

Running alongside
Men, chasing golden
Droplets, wearies us.

Even in no-birth
Feminine nature
Is of creator:
Communities made,
Held and supported,
Loving all critters.

Love does not belong to God.
It is you who are.

Woman, hear me now.
You are artist.
Come back together
And create.

Tools

Brainless, timeless art
Plastic-held ink, innocent.
Are you hiding, God?

There Is A God

In recovering myself as an artist
I discovered permission to accept a 'God'
That I had previously seen as not the smartest
Way to live; a force I had outlawed.

Dissolving my internal barrier
Has shown me the Way.
Without it, I realise, I am half a being:
Someone for whom *all* is muscle,
Never making hay,
But instead all *effort*,
Clouding creation,
Chasing the beautiful Muse away.

Reconnecting with the Force really is Forceful.
It stops that fragmenting feeling
That makes creator life just awful.

It's Not Brain

You cannot muscle
Birth, nor can you muscle art.
Become the River.

Erasure

What is this Thing that
Is held under glorious spotlight,
Revered and isolated;
Held, as a benchmark,
An endpoint,
A limitation,
That stops you from being
"Good",
That crushes your process,
That fails to support you in
Your joyful endeavours
Creating what is needed by
Humanity *now*?

Oh, that Thing.
That glossy, careful, prized
Ruler that measures creation
Against some arbitrary
Past meaning of *Art*,
Kept on a pedestal by a
Society whose connexion
With the exoteric
Has become esoteric, isolated,
And revered because of its
Failure to recognise that
We all are Tall.

What is this Thing.
Held against which You are measured
And to which You bring your
Paltry artefact for recognition,
As if you could match
Four hundred years' worth of
Artistic devolution, destruction

By a thousand drips of
Water eating through gods and
Divinity and family and
Femininity,
Patterned on a social experiment
That says
Mother doesn't matter—

Here is real art, a
Man perfectly rendered,
When in fact Man is created in perfection,
Rendered in its wholeness
Three hundred times a minute
By those for whom
Histories are never written.

For while they are the victors
This world is working to
Erase them.

In Wholeness We Are Saved

Curl your warm fingers
Around my one,
Show me the window and
Sing a non-language song
That only I understand.

Raw,
Unfiltered experience shining
Through eyes unshuttered and free,
Staring soulfully into me,
Teaching me how to stay
       Present.
I recover slowly,
An addict led astray by
Self, society and
Well-intentioned, misled Others.

If I take each seed-bearing
Goddess by the hand
To show her the window;

If I sing her a hopeful
Song in the non-language
That only I know;

Can I gift her
This same orchid of the flame?

How many inner children
Could we save
If they, too, recognised
       Their art?
Confronting,
The realities of birth

Are not of Mind,
Are
        Raw.

Unearthing more than
That occult gateway
You return me to my heart,
To the locus of all creation
With every electrifying touch.

In recovery,
My artist makes her home
In that same
Soulful place.

Mothers are makers,
Divinity's creators,
Yet where so many fight
A battle
For selfdom and light
There need only be
        Recognition:

Completeness,
Hidden inside that soft, small moment
When you wrap your warm
Little fingers
Around my one
And tug me to the window
So I can see.

Heeding The Call

In light chats with the mum in law
Artist by life and trade
I heard sev'ral time mention
Of a book, *The Artist's Way*.

She dropped it O so casually
I missed it many times
Until the muse whispered to me:
'What's that? Please go and find.'

I'd spent the best of a year or more
Attempting to define
Just what I came to learn was that
I'd ignored my artist's cries.

She'd been ignored, I'd shut her up
So this was her new style,
To get the art to come to me
By dint of others' smiles.

So I asked my mum by marriage
What was this magic book
I found it on that very day
And on my Kobo put.

Imagine my great surprise when then
The intro through I read,
This book it seems was wrote for me,
My art was nearly dead!

I'd noticed what my heart had said
I followed her to Source
And now the flow is coming loose
Unblocked and gushing forth.

If I had not heard the call
This subtle, ringing cry,
I'd still be feeling stuck and sad,
Divorced and wondering why.

It's not priority that shifts
When kids light up your life,
It's awakening of artistry,
A new, amazing life.

There are others who create with you,
But ignore 'co-creation' trends
As the mum you know it's all on you:
The portal, door, not men!

You take on board their DNA
You wait and bake and prop
When they emerge so do you,
But equally new, that's what.

It's scary to find paths to truth;
Difficult alone:
So take my hint and know in you,
The artist is your home.

Artist In Recovery: Act 1

Hung up on structure
Hampered by 'story'
The artist whimpers,
Struck back into hiding.

Freed from her shackles
Bindings and pain
The phantoms still bite her,
The fear worse than the pain.

In facing her freedom
She locks up her plan,
Gets knotted in plots
Ideas? Ha! A sham.

Her natural inklings
Appear not to be
Anything useful,
When mapped A through B.

So if structure is code
But art is Divine
Where is the mode
That makes it all mine?

Artist In Recovery: Act Two

It wasn't until I began to rant
On pages lined in inky blue
With pen in hand and brain asleep
That I began to heal.

Addicted to a story fake,
Told times uncounted in years unlived
I'd shoved the artist in a bag
Therewith to wilt and die.

The pen is mighty, will blunt a sword,
Held loosely its power rings and burns;
Connect to heart and Earth, a channel
Filled high and full.

Twelve steps they say is all it takes:
Accept divinity's shining grace,
A major feat for godless woman
Faithless, solo, alone.

Imagine then my greatest shock
To see beneath the fen-filled land
Muddy and murky and gassy and wet
Cut up bricks of peat.

Carefully excavate the past
Examine it unjudged, and quiet
Focus and question-filled mind enquires
How the jail grew.

A wall, a brick, some dust and blood
Preserved to tell an inky tale
Of self-defeat, abuse and loss,
Nasty hurtful past.

With guidance, clarity, courage and pen
I wrote and felt new feelings, clear
Of mind, a curious stake in this
Recovery.

I learned that things of gate and gall
Were needed in the pride-filled fall
That woman I was once before
Is gone, here I stand.

I'm feeble, yes, vanilla too
A fledgling artist, my skin is new
I have to relearn how to walk:
Fall, get up again.

We cannot gift our children us
Unless we grow and nurture us.
Our artists must come first, it's time.
I can: So can you.

Liminal Woman I

You tell yourself
That you were forged in fire
When all that happened
Was that you dropped
The veil on reality
And encountered the You
Who exists in Nature.

Liminal Woman II

Dancing in the veiled light a ghostly fluid figure
A spirit loose and free to move in ever growing vigour
Blind perhaps from futureness, absent forward sight
Cast alone in present space, childlike delight.
Forcefields of reality dissolved, just now they've gone
Leaving her true nature only, raw pink rising dawn.
Lost inside a fuzzy time, mindless heart-based place
Her dancing silvers gleeful air, joyful graceful face.

You Got It

Art is luxury:
It feels warm, peaceful and calm.
Free of binds, and mind.

Woman's Time Is Cyclic

Examining the days
We see each one different.

Birthed the same,
Not any one the same.

The wind, water, smells, sounds, light.
The clouds, trees, insects, birds.
The animals, humans, systems, structures.

Each is uniqe to Today.

And Today.

And Today.

So how do we relate Today to Today
Or Tomorrow with Now
Or Then with Hence?

We don't.

Instead, we see.

We listen.

We know.

Whispers Make Art

Unfold the darkness to
Discover sense-making apparatus
Long since buried;
Rusted in torrid salt air,
Sharp on the tongue,
Difficult to digest,
Hardwoods rotted giving life
In a new era
That you are not required to understand.

Just listen!

Get out of the way,
Cease your exusings and musings
To act:
For this train will appear
In the fog
And it will hit you
Unless a sparkle catches
Your eye, and You,
In your new-found innocence,
Allow yourself to be led.

Heartness

Visioning isn't manifesting,
Yet so many women fall into
The trap of trying to muscle
The things that their hearts create.

The moment they get out of the Way
For art is her art
And her art is her heart
So being present is the gift.

The vortex in the cycle is
In the moment
Of creation—
If only she would listen,

Follow,

Do.

Fire Orchid

Hidden beneath the Earth's top soil
Lies a quiet being of root and oil
Ignited when a flame alights
Dancing in her twinkling lights.

A black and red and royal hue
Linking her and me and you,
Shining in a realm of veil
Becoming She from top to tail.

Fire lights, a burning way,
Begins to crackle, swish and sway,
Raising ever-smoky heights
To skylines new and tree-tops bright.

The burning torches light the way
From caverns dark to peaks of day,
Pushing you to realms unseen
But felt and clawed, its calling means

You'll never stray when once you hear
That trumpet call, that voice so clear.

It whispers deep, it whispers wild:

Follow me, artistic child.

Body

Body mine, you heal
Rifts gone, grass baskets woven;
Clear water yields fish.

Mind

No time, no time, no—
Moments are gifts, useful all:
Don't wonder, just do.

Spirit

In an evergreen land
"Spring" is "waft".
New smells and changed song
Herald a calling   .
That elsewhere must awaken:
Subtlety asks for attention.

The Artist Lives

It takes time for the artist
To recover.
Discovered sitting on the debris
Of the fallen chamber,
The prison that held her
Captive and silent,
She is vulnerable and soft.
Her body ghostly pale from
Years of darkness,
Her muscles atrophied by disuse,
Her eyes blinded,
Cloudy,
Taking time to cope with light again.
See her tears streaming down her face:
What is grief?
What is pain?
What is a consequence of seeing again?
It's all some kind of overflow
With which not to concern yourself.
Your only task is care.
Your only job to nurture.
To pick up this skittish, abused puppy
And cover her with love,
Because love is the way to growth.
Not shame, nor fear, nor anger.
Yet she and ye will
RAGE
Until the storms pass.

When the giant tides ebb away
You'll be wizened, creased by
Coarse salt air,
And she will have her sea legs,
Capable of standing, dancing while

Sailing through each and every current.

You, darling woman,
Trapped in old thinking
Feel more like the caged animal.
The freer she becomes
The more you pace,
Seeing this life is not the old life,
Seeing the consequence of
Mum-dom
Is that Time feels elusive,
That you're working for others,
That society calls you back to
Its sickened and diseased
Falseful state of "existing" in dubious ways.

… And now this?
Rest easy; she is you.
Caring for you is caring for her;
Nurturing her nurtures your world
And at some point
You'll understand the
Immensity of snatches of time
Turned to productive use,
You'll grasp the enormity of the moments of Art
The allowing of whatever God
Creates your Muse.

Until finally your artist is
Walking with you,
Whispering in your ear,
And You—to your credit—
Take notes.

How To Art

When music plays,
Dance!
Even if it appears when you're doing something else.

When people play,
Watch!
Then you can join them in their fun.

When animals play,
Follow!
For you are also one and they are family.

Formula

The structure is stuck like glue,
Informing a fear of failure
What can I do?

I'll write this poem in form
A structure that gives a shape
Write and learn.

The first scene reflects the end
So write it last—it depends!
Wait and see.

The theme is a statement or dialogue
A comment thrown out in foreshadow
Not a big deal.

The setup is fun, it explores this world
Like B but it's A and skatee
Enjoy the ride.

A catalyst breaks the idyll
It shakes and it breaks
        …. BORED.

Too much formula, not enough free.

Faith

Inside your heart is
Perfection, if you trust it.
Not sure? Then dive! Dive!

Tree of Life

Fey handed up a curious button that
At her mere touch sprang up into flower, then
Shrank to a ball, all shiny and round
Ribbed like a walnut, a heavy gold prize.
Whispering low, as she breathed out her words, our
Woman spoke. '…seed?' with a frown on her brow.

'Yes!' giggled Fey, dancing 'round in a jig, tiny
Bows falling off in a heap at its feet.
'Go find the map,' and pointed a finger
T'wards the west where the sun was faltering clearer.
Time had just gone, in a flash, in a shake, and
Woman then panicked, dropped the seed in her lap.

Moody confusion, for out on her walk she had
Gone—who knows where? The day was all gone and the
Park was gone too: In place now was a
Weird all-grey that twinkled a lot, but
Going home now seemed like asking too much, and
All that she had was a seed and an order

Asking her only to march to that quarter.
What could she do beyond screaming self blue? Was
There a choice or was this It, that she do?
Hesitating on the brink of no choice, it
Seemed really hard to find her own voice.

Squished as she was by being in nowhere, she
Nodded and chirrupted, 'Well, sure, I'll go there,'
Leaving behind that funny little fella.
Paths opened up to left and to right, the
Woman grew confused about which one was right but she
Kept one eye on the oft-setting sun, which

Bobbled and wobbled and popped up more than once.
Smack! A wall appeared, its face she
Hit, and, falling, whimpered 'shit!'
Chest first on the featureless ground she
Fumbled, scared of losing the seed.
Sitting up, and dusting off, the

Woman saw stars, the sun now gone its
Place was took by lights anew, and
As she witness, she then saw
Movement in stars became a note, a
Map of sorts, a scratchy thing that
Told her to keep this seed growing—but

No instructions, nothing else, just
Light all gone and blindness felt.
Wait! A smell, a piney thing, of
Vanilla warm, stirring; she
Rubbed her eyes the better to see and
Still saw nothing clear or free, in-

Stead a shadow, looming large, a
Stand of pink indeterminate size. What
Could she have done the woman wondered
Making her walk this crazy nightmare,
Pixie-led for sure, a fateful thing that
Meant her work was suffering. And

Now this madness. What to do? Just
Take a seed and hope? How cruel! Then
Suddenly a sound of sticks being
Crunched under big feet. The
Woman's breath came short and fast, her
Fear took over and nausea passed, shedding.

Scooted back as if to find a
Haven, a wall, a solid shelter to

Hide in, to sleep in, to wait for the sun to
Rise—but nothing she found; the crunching
Louder now, the thing almost on her!
Eyes appeared like large moony saucers; a

Body and claws and wings soon after. It
Bellowed and yowled and raised its fists high—the
Woman reacted with arms to the sky; in
Hiding her face was all she could do, and
Cowering low she made herself small but
Creature drew nearer until she was sure that

Death was close by. And then it was gone.
Fluttering down in glittering drops fell
Letters that formed in a note on the ground. They
Spelled out instructions, if that's what they be, a
Riddle that felt impossible to see:

From her you must walk in a circular way
Feeling hot feeling lost feeling sad for your loss
In the dark you'll be blind you'll hear not and you'll find
That Seed grows a lot gets heavy and you'll fall
In chasm and on cliff top in river and in shoal
No guide, no maps, no compass you'll find
Just You help You the Youness of y'r mind.
So stand and march and know that the fire
Is waiting and burning and smoking signal-less-ize.

Fury it held her in momentous grasping, she
Pulled out the seed, its glittering sparkle, its
Golden outside all glossy and new, but
Flinging it far felt like all she could do! What
Madness was here, why now, why her? Such
Stupidness seemed a bad trip gone mad. She

Roared at the sky, fists raised up in balls tight
Rage-filled inchoate, a trembling soul that

Knew of no option but onwards to go and
Failed to see what God sought to show her.
Light faded. Suddenly left in the dark, the
Woman was startled, rage fading fast. In

Alarm she strained eyes more to see than was wise, and
Sat, pricked up ears, yet hearing gone too.
Pocketing Seed she felt for a stick, the
Better for which to feel on her way. The
Path it had edges, a faint rolling feel of
Pebble and gravel, friction by feel. Found one

Upstanding she scraped with the stick,
Barely she felt edge, enough to unstick her-
Self from the ground, venturing forth in
Darkness and quiet but not quite in fear.

Air grew colder the further she walked, as
Damp smell and musty, leaves rot under foot, of
Creek lines and sunless, of layers of fall, of
Canopy stretching afar and up tall.

Gravel gave way to soft moss replete with
Scattering leaves cushioning her sore feet, the
Seed grew too big for her pocket and holds, so
She carried it hand-wise the precious cargo.

'I can't feel the path,' she whispered aloud, she
Threw down the stick in disgruntlement and
Hugged close the seed, small comfort it made, its
Size now beyond a single-hand-grip. The

Further she walked, the deeper her grief in
Losing her place, her importance, her keep! It
All felt so far gone, a life lived afar, of
Hustling forward, of fighting for life.

Tears freely falling, her nose blocked by snot, she
Wept as she walked in the darkness, no words in her
Mouth; if words she had had, no ears would they
Fill, isolated and broken she limped on

Towards some goal she'd not planned, an arrival, a
Quest that found her, chose her to go on, a
Keeping of promise both loved and forlorn, but
Grief wrapped her tight hugged her in its warmth as

Seed threw out love that kept her on her
Feet and in hope, refuelling her bleed, some
Crazy emanation on which she'd feed, it
Gave her a sense and a sight came to bloom,

Eyeless and mindless a heart-felt-led move-
Ment in her soul, embers come to life; it
Blew them from a gentle waft-giving life, and
Light in the depths glowing pearly and orange.

Drying her tears as they welled from the source,
Embers grew tendrils that tied her to Seed, that
Wove into heart and skin and spine, cre-
Ating a one-ness, built new in delight.

The further she walked, the stronger it grew, it
Faded away her feelings of blue and
Came to a place that was all filled with love, our
Woman forgot who she was or what she was

Supposed to be, until something
Whispered, 'Stay for a mo',' and she
Felt an edge-drop with tips of her toes.
Recoiling in horror from brink of disaster
Scurried back quicker than Jesus could master.

Flick head around to eyeball that voice, she

Finds no-one there, just darkness, no sight
Scratching the ground, a foot showed her clear:
Deafness persists! No voice in her ear!

Closing her eyes, she breathed out real slow,
Began to be led by a heart-voice so low,
Shuffling near to the cliff-edge she sat
Dumping her legs into voice, seed in lap.

Cold fear filled her from toes through to head
Breathing through the heavy cold dread, the
Feeling that all gone, lost, all done *still*. It was
Thickest right here, even path gone to ground.

Waiting for something to strike her a light, she
Shuffled bum slowly around to the right, the
Seed weighed a ton, prevented smooth moves,
Exhausting to bumble in dust on the edge, but
Somehow she knew it was not to be solved, that
Down was way forwards! But how?

'Jump,' kissed the breeze that tickled her face,
'Death is your equal in this frightening place.'
Hammering heart beating up in her mouth, she
Clenched both hands on the edge of the cliff.

Swing her legs up and—stayed still. Oh, fear!
Without tears to shed, absent more angst, she
Flat-felt her soul, empty, opaque,
Meaningless name, empty of salt, she

Closed her blind eyes
Held her breathed
Hugged her seed
And

Jumped.

Dawn broke.
Pink.
Cloudless.

Curled around in spinning formation, the
Woman hugged close a golden seed to
Which she'd bonded, rooting together
Deep into Earth, no creature of two
Formed yet new, singular twin,
Warm together, dawning dew fresh.

Comfortable now with her place,
Becoming part of forest's green space
Love rooted deep into sweet dark Earth;
Shooting, blooming, growing a space of

Hers, her own, selfishly sharing the
Beat of her heart, nourished, caring
Drawing on hidden mysteries many
Shiftless and endless, expansion of Gods, she's

Tickled by others, roots who find her,
Sharing their lessons through secretive messengers
Unknown to walkers of path passing yonder
Expanded yet still, ageless eternity.

Herewish she grows in unison bold into
Towering roadmaps kissing the sky, with
Little one close feeling tangled and fly, bliss-
Ful and fulsome, needing nothing else.

Casting an eye here and there roundabout
Path passing yonder gave her a shiver, for she
Saw a woman, harried and cross, out
Walking swiftly muttering about her boss, with
Shocked realisation she knew it was She!

Existing in two strands, two lives, but now
One blind to life, other in creation
Simultaneity caused ground to shift.

Facing her face with its fears found a rift, a
Wound unforeseen and unknown and deep is
Seen; made it close, a veil brought right down for-
Ever past gone, that showy life with its

Bosses and stresses and mildew inside,
Relinquished for this, entanglement true,
Real life rooted in not one but two.

Seeing is feeling is moving through those tough
Moments blind and deaf and not shown nor
Mapped—but instinct, it has a compass;
Sextant, stars take their turns in whispering
Directions, for if you listen you will be led.
Darkness is where you find your own light, not
Given or handed but trusted insight, it's
You trusting you led by something much greater than
Accepting whatever comes out of the grate, for
Creation is constant and art filled with doubt, so for-
Get what you know or you want and find out.

Artist

The mountain calls us
See vistas, over, over
Round and round, is art.

Be Led

Familiar
Landscape numbs us to beauty
Wait. Stop. Listen close.

Messages on wind
Sunshine warming hardened hearts
One word for green-blue.

Seven seasons here
Ancient land shifts by subtlety
Turn off your tee vee.

Adventure forth now
Learn the smells, the calls, the clouds,
Become the teacher.

Learn by being One;
Capture knowledge—not for you.
Draw, dance, sing, perform.

Western happiness
Forbidden, like artist life,
It's all just legend.

Internal guidance
All your lives talking at once,
Wait. Stop, Listen close.

Sea Spotting

The ocean has moods
That tell us of things to come:
Rain.
Earthquake.
Tsunami.
Hot weather.
Attuning oneself requires
Vision.
Attention.
Memory.
In the same way your
Art has moods
That divine the weather
And reflect your
Inner life.
Ripples from butterfly wings,
Beaten for just a day
Then gone,
Yet with implications
That resonate
Through lifetimes.

Fashion

If binning old socks
Was part of your art degree:
Sweet jasmine breeze. Smell!

Magic Pages

Magic pages sing
Unconscious songs of pure joy
Lifting, breathing, Be;
Into worldly shape. You see
This is where you're s'posed to be.

Homecoming I

Slipping softly
Through warmed rooms familiar,
Daily mods bonding
With soul's dust scattered floor-side.
Magic in every sneeze.

Houses of love
Fill corners with webbed friends
Chasing direct food scraps
Whose existence is mere
Nourishment of yesterday.

Let it all slide.
Finding moments to play
Between meals half-made
Flow, flow into buckets
That, spilling, become gems

Shining silver
Motes of treasured sparkle
Chase them, eat them, laugh!
This is the origin.
This is where (he)art begins.

Uh, really?

Mums are those people
Who are responsible?
Seriously. Fun.

Homecoming II

Painting rainbows
With each pen-stroke, newly
Crafted in time's flows
Healing generations
Warmed by the kitchen-side.

The hearth matters
Even where roles shift, change,
Anchored safely, here,
Where hugs are plenty and
Infants teach boundless love.

You did not know,
Had not a single clue
How deep beauty runs.
How connected we are,
How human we can be.

That empty life
Filled with interests yet
Obliterated
By witnessing one kiss
Freely given by child

Who knows no rule
No restraint on kindness
No conflicting voice
Making him hesitate,
Vibrating in heart wisdom.

Allow filling,
Become the spring, welling
Out of breaking rock

To spill and cleanse away
Ancient gut, ancient time.

Mist refracting
Reminds us of ourselves
Split into boxes
Whose coherence melted,
Who finds self back at home.

Walk Alone Again

Rediscovering
What is meant by mind-space,
Bathe in clear water.

Little Hands

Holding hands, heart melts.
If only you'd known how deep
Love runs, flowing true.

Hold the Tiny Hand

The roadmap to enlightenment
Is laced through your body,
Pumpted from vein to ventricle,
Powered by a force unseen,
Unknown, mistrusted
Until you are held palm to palm
With a being whose
Existence is untarnished by
Expectation and limitation.

That moment when his roadmap
Links to yours,
You feel it in the very centre
Of the place that enables you to feel
… in heart patterns,
Recognised in this life
But existing for millenia,
In a deeply rooted network of
Theoretical mychorrizal energy
Connecting all:

Until you encounter
That spark that throws you
To the boundary of your existence
And reminds you of who you are
You're a forgotten shard of
Isolation.

Untrauma

Shedding skins, onion
Layers hidden to the light
Which shines to glisten
Not as bloodied wounds this time.
Could this be healing and growth?

Don't Be So Literal, Mum

Walking with you
On those first sure-footed
Journeys into the world
You remid me that
The path is
Not the way to discovery.

Art Heals

If physical work
Antidotes mental trauma;
If an artist's work
Heals the soul of humanity;
Then your art heals you and Us.

I Want to Sing For You

I want to sing a song for you
Of rain that fell, of plants that grew,
Of breezes warm and jasmine sweet
Of learning how our bodies meet
In ways unseen, in soulful touch,
In waves that speak of oh so much.

I want to sing and paint a scene
Of people passing, pasts unseen,
Whose natures cause averted eyes
And frightened hugs 'til you pass by
That tells me more about your soul
Than any confession you could have told.

I want to share this deep I know
Of mother-child connected role
That sings non-language, plays a game
So hard for others to come and play,
That simple insight new and true
That speaks through us, is Me and You.

I want to help you start to see
What we've been missing, you and me,
This life so full of love and care
That we had shunned and wouldn't share
This force that melts the hardest hearts
Is primal, godlike, it's not apart.

I want to teach you what I've learned
Becoming mother, life upturned,
Its cyclic being, centrifuge
That forges Now, its turns a fugue:
Recurring spiral, golden mean,
Mathematics all, spirit clean.

I want to draw a picture clear
To show the sacred smell of hair
Soft and pillowy, grown anew
Tickles the nose, a musky hue
That never ages or fades away
Just changes, deepens, day to day.

I want my art to give you pause
Reflecting on this journey, 'cause
My heart reels in every mo'
I want to share it with you so, but
I fear you won't care or see
How meaningful it is to me.

Or what it could perhaps teach you
Or show you now what life can do
For your sore heart, its empty vase
That yearns for scentful flowers large.
And so I scrawl, I write in vain.
Perhaps my art could do the same.

Poison

A poison drips slow,
Misdirecting attention:
Screen-sugar soul-theft.

Listen

Listening, I'm led
Through walls of fear, anxious, bled
Out until you fill
This movement; gentle, willing,
Put your brain aside.

I Sold My Soul

I made a pact,
I made a deal,
No devils here:
Just pure goodwill.
But still the power
Of contract
Supports the deal,
Signs the pact.
I'll do the work
And you, you Thing
Will make it work,
You'll make it sing:
Did I sell
My soul to thee?
Well yes, I did—
But questions rear
If I am me
And you are you
Is *soul* a thing
Or simple truth?

Seasons

If seasons were just
Dates on a calendar, then
Prediction is an
Easy matter; right, now kids!
Life is an ocean: Deep, wild.

This holds true for you.
This holds true for your weather.
Stagnate, suffocate:
Water sans life or oxygen
Dies a stinking 'death', yet feeds.

Because life goes on,
Death is a transformation;
Energy moved, used—
Why then feeble human must
You insist things stay the same?

This flux is power.
Inside its movement, create
Heartfelt, beautiful
Moments that bring joy to life:
Joy for you and your family.

Creativity
Has no seasonality
Don't wait until it's 'right':
Art has no season; just Now:
Breathe. Trust. Go forth and make.

Draw! Antonio, draw!

If ever you
Doubt your ability
To draw, paint, sculpt, make,
Write, sing, dance, film, bake, sew, play—
Listen! Master artists
Tell us one thing:
Draw! Antonio, draw!
Revel in the process,
Slay those dragons of doubt
And with their scales
You shall build an edifice
Worthy of Michaelangelo himself.

-ness.

Just at that moment
When doubt has you by the throat,
Cast your eyes to the sky.
Recall that this foreverness
Is but a moment.
It, too, shall pass.
And in the moment-by-moment
Cascading, you will discover
That doubt is mere
Hesitation,
A glitch in the faith
That allows you to predict sunrise.

Occulting.

Real artists are those
Whose process creates by-product
That obscures process
But who understand "by-product"
Is only what others see.

Live From the (he)art

Let go of your art.
Burn your bridges to Sanity,
Slaughter your darlings in the pale light of the risen moon,
Cast from your fingertips the effervescent spirit, woven into
senseless and sensory delights.
Cavort in the glory of foolishness,
Revel as only you can in the cheesy muck of goofiness that
shrieks but never insists on Being Good, and
Allow art to dance her way into the world,
Elevated into new position by the sheer joy of being made.
Release that ghastly need to be
Serious, the
Killer of all aspirations,
Driving beige boredom forever onwards.

Let go of your art.
Dance naked in the waning fire of knowledge burned in pyres,
Sing loudly in languages not yet known,
Hail that great creator of madness,
That crazy witching whose depth is unknown,
Plumbed only to raise little devils for the edification of the
Mortals who tread in
Fear,
Disallowing themselves the sheer
Glee of creating because life isn't like that.

Let your art live.
Embrace the anxiety of process,
Trudge the neverending back woods to the darkness that holds
your secrets, and
Scale the epic, uplifting mountain
In imaginative and uplifting ways
That you can't place.

For this is how life
Must be lived
If lived truly,
Deeply,
Madly.

Studio Time

Lying in the dark
Listening to gentle breath
I become Artist.

Stars

Recognise
That welling pool
Shimmering as its currents
Rise.

Notice—
That stars aren't only in the sky.
They dance over rocks,
Sparkling beneath
Bubbles that also dance.

Who knew that above and below
Could be so literal,
Coexisting,
Filling us with a wonder
About all things.

And in this wonder,
New possibilities take root.

It's Not Easy Getting Dirty

Small patent shoes and
Ankle socks walk
Gently down the muddy path;
Careful,
Lest the stones and muck
Flick up and dirty that
Pretty tan and ivory shoe.
Following the trail down into
Cool, damp, forest clearing,
Speckled light glowing
Through shuffling leaves and
A babbling brook curving its
Way through rocks that
Eventually yield their shapes…
Notice
That you can pass by,
An observer,
But it's those dirty workboots
Who trudge past you,
Coated in the wet mud of
Deeper tracks
Who have seen landscapes
You will never see,
Tasted air you'll never feel,
And become one with the places
Whose spirit patterned deep
Into the soul's scrapbook
That experience the
Fullness of life.
So you,
You! The one who is afraid of
The murk,
Remove those shoes.
Allow your toes to sink deep

Into the shaley mud,
Feel that spring push your feet
Into crevices you can't yet see,
And when you do,
Feel the richness of life
Compel you.
Listen to what it tells you,
And, taking it,
Allow yourself to become it,
A materiel of destruction
Leaving behind
Beauty,
Goodness,
Energy and fire,
Ignited to warm the
Atmosphere we know as
Humanity.

Music is Everywhere

Rippling rocks turn
Percussion under-wave action;
Endless symphony.

Terra Scintillant

The moment I saw
Golden stars dancing in pools:
Was it upside-down?

Bubbling Celebrity

If stars are caused by bubbles
Dancing across rocks under water
Then where are the bubbles that
Shine galaxies into our lives?

Sleepless Artist

Stealing from sleep-time
Moving ink through torch light, dark
Moments in. And out.

Run Like a River

The greatest lie is
That artists toil solo in
An ecstasy, alone.
Who chose that story? Believe
Only that you're a channel.

Are You Afraid of the Dark?

Darkness.
Whisper, *oh dark, dark.*
Concealer of known and unknown
Feeling lost
Trapped in this unenlightened place
That shows us who we are.

That reflects
And fills
Every orifice with a
Pressure unbearable.

Darkness
Enables us.
It makes our feet itch to travel
Moving somewhere,
Anywhere,
Away from here until we find the light.

Darkness
Feels like emptiness.
Ignorance,
A pathless unknown,
Forcing our knowledge out and
Away from us,
Hiding, like the feet we trust to
Carry us.

Darkness is
Essential.
In it we nurture our selves
Come to find our roots
Trust the gentle winds that
Toss us to and fro.

Until
Dawn breaks.
We feel it before we see,
Hear the subtle shifts in
Birdsong, paint
Colourful boundaries around
Our worlds until

Suddenly, turning,
The light blinds us.
          How is this any different
From
the Dark?

Plateau

Long, flat, empty place
Atop a rise
Of some kind.
Set foot to march the mountain pass,
A-weight with things to make it nice
Around the path a steady climb
The mountain is hidden beneath dense clouds
So all you can see is plateau jutting proud
Jutting near then far beneath misty cloud

Desiring to reach this you treble your pace
Tripping along in fire and haste
Then you reach it.
It's empty.

Mountain soars up.
Wander around,
Catch your breath.
Gaze up.

Plateau is no challenge,
Excitement is gone,
One-foot, one-foot,
Rest, gaze, breathe, think.

So far left to go.

Now this, a test!

Reach it you will
Lean in quick I'll tell you a secret well-kept:
Plateau feels like void but is teeming with life!

Accept the rest,

Regain your strength
Peer close feel the magic
Bring you to life.

When time is right pick up your pack,
Trudge on up hill and

Never look back.

Heart Song (language)

In a place far away
Found by space, found by time, I
Met a people just like me
But unlike me they could see.

They had a song, sung by heart,
Uniting them, creating art,
It was a song, sung by heart,
In a language we all forgot.

Hand on heart from one to one,
It was a song that I was taught
That felt like ecstasy,
And when I knew, then I could see

That this place that we all seek
Is not out there, is not in Space,
It's in your deep, your quiet mind,
The place you go until you find

Not the peace that others promise
Not the nothing void of black
But connection, forgotten language
Of the heart song that lets you make.

Nurture

Once you've gathered
Your broken artist in
Your arms, and
Wrapped her wounds,
Sung gentle songs to ease her fear,
Cuddled and warmed and
Rocked and bathed,
You must nourish her,
Suckle her, feed her—with
Fun, sun, colour, dance,
Play time.
Give her the honour of
Daily time, of weekly dates.
Show her that love is endless and everlasting, and
In return she will enrich your life in
Ways immense, immeasurable.
The only thing she requires of you is that
You keep the door open and
Say 'yes'.

Golden Mean

Mothering's quiet
Secret power resides in
Continuous unfolding.

Energy ebbs, flows,
Fills all the spaces with life;
Journeys never end.

Frustration rises
Expectations like planning;
Step forward, unseeing.

In life lived as art
Turned away from narrative,
Embrace your darkness.

Each discovery
Equally impressive; new
Sounds, heart-wise, call you.

No peak can be reached.
Each towers above the other.
Find rest in plateau.

This hidden knowledge
Weaving sisters together
Spirals, not circles.

Time is not linear;
Nurturing art is mothering
Water eddies, wears down rocks.

Embrace continuity.
Be always in the moment.

This is destination.

Transfixed

Transfixed,
I am heart and eyes
For you.
Submerged as we are,
Learning to dismember
Anxiety and befriend Fear,
Sparkling bubbles delight
You; and I don't see them.
But in my not-seeing
I understand that our
Destiny
Is
To
Rise.

Stolen

When taking stock of
Prolific youthful output
I saw you took half.
Half of art is half of me—
Revenge is a dish served cold.

Redefine "Art"

Art is not 'artist';
Art is living intention,
Mindful moments, all.
Ideas of art being 'output'
Misdirect you from your source.

Early crazies

Daddy's girl became
Business woman; tell self lies
Like, 'this too is art'.

Pearls Are Not Wisdom

Stories we hear make
Impressions carved layers deep.
Is that bone or scar?

Listening, we make
New lives built from others' lies,
Oyster-like, held peak.

Directing our lives,
Forceful waters push us fast,
Hold tight to the pretty.

Imagine freedom
Possibility steals beneath
Release the tension.

Close your eyes, sit quiet
Move past fearing the unknown.
Can you stand free-fall?

Unravelling guilt
Allows beauty to rest here
Emerging from you.

Others' stories make
Generational pathways;
Art is trusting yours.

First Trust

Trusting self, courage
Needed here. Gird your loins. Stand!
Toddle. Toddle. Walk.

Drip, drip, drop.

Some say
That your weeping nose as you write
Is the emergence of
A font of grief,
Inner crying,
Released as the tension
Dissipates on ink-scrawl.
Or, it could just be the cold.

An Addict's Treasury

Addicted to
Tales told
Of lives I lived
Both young and old,

I backed my way
To a stagnation
Empty work
Without cessation.

Releasing this
Was hard to do
I wept a river
Worked spellcraft, too.

But what I didn't know
Was what became
A magic show.

Gifted me
From creator's source
A little boy
A code (not Morse)

That shifted me
And shifted you
To this strange place
Of treasures new.

With it I found
The tales false
An addict's lie
An endless waltz

With others' stories
And others' dreams
When this right here
Helped me find me.

The change was hard
It stripped me bare
Demanding, asked,
Why do you care?

The truth it came
Like hidden moon
Rays outstretched
A glowing ruin.
I didn't much
So then I wrote
New tales of mine
Not learned, not rote

Instead coherence
Came to me;
Because of you,
I learned to see.

Have you seen this girl?

Why recover art?
You replaced 'joyful' with 'Good?'
Sanity goes missing.

Processing

In the time
That it takes
To feel bad
Cos you suck
You can draw
You can paint
You can love what you've done.
In the pace
Of this place
Just for you
Not for fame
You can make
You can take
You can lose that frightful pace
That you hold
That there pen
To the fold
You can shine
You can scribe
You can be joyful mind
So just be now
Be that kid
With closed and knitted brow
You will feel
You will see
This was always meant to be.

An Endangered Species

In darkening the door of
Modernity's narrative we find
An endless mess, a
Carnage
Of all that nowheres us.
Scattered, like bowls cast
Hastily aside in an effort
To abandon all that
Got us from there to here.
When the home-fire dies out
The bone-chilling cold
Cannot be out-cast,
Meals become subsistence snacking and
The comforts of communal
Gathering fade into the dusty
Songs sung by generations past,
Unkept by those who tally the Victory.
For even in the twilight, it serves no master.
Stay,
Stay true to your gentle nature,
Allow yourself to return home
Wrapped warmly in the
Love forged by billions of
Hearts now and always,
Carried
As if by luminescent wildlings
Sparkling palm to palm,
Eye to eye,
Heart to heart,
Reimagining the sacredness of
Woman,
Whose deep and
Soular connection with life
Cannot be extinguished in a

Hasty dash to a 'better' place.
For while we sing and tidy,
Cook and nourish,
Grow and make,
We are weaving together the strands of
New creatures alive and still,
Who each grow in time,
Who bond us still.

Sanity

When next you feel a
Poison mood, ask who's fighting.
Have you played today?

The Kettle, It Whistles Loudly

Locked inside that skin of yours
Are journeys long and tales told
Of ways to be and who does what
Just art is never there.

In sighing ways, 'it must be nice
To have a luxurious life
One fuelled with time and inspiration
To make the art for cultivation
Of that talent you've got there'…

Is it any wonder moods go
Swinging wildly up-down-to-fro
In the failure to recognise
The spiritual enterprise
That keeps you rooted there?

Musicians playing to feel better,
Painters always-drawing's tempers
Levelled out through crafting process
Will be the first to kneel and profess
Art keeps sanity there.

It's a sign that you're not keeping
To the honourable way of meeting
Your artist's health and healing
When your sanity wobbles, teetering
Because of that life that you've got there.

So my advice to you by illustration
Is to listen to that deep frustration
It's a sign, needed recreation
So saddle up that burning passion,
Let it go, now, right, there.

You're A Genius

They say genius
Is crazy, that artists are too:
Art is genius?
With no imagination
Anything novel is crazed.
      Allow this nonsense
No entry to the sacred
Temple of your mind—
It takes root and festers black,
Swallowing all in its path.
      Keep your hackles up,
Lest poisonous people drag
You into Mundane,
Where magic is myth, folklore,
And life is coloured beige. Ugh.

Cairngorm

Survival: beauty
On high, attracting insects
So why so much grey?

Primal Truth

Whose attention do you seek
When all your energy goes out
To caring for someone else?

Whose love do you yearn for
When all the loving feeds
So much one way?

Whose life is it you lead
When all the doing is caring,
Exhaustion and fray?

Who do you turn to
When life is so full
And every moment swings by like a fool?

How do you nurture
That one thing
That one love
That beautiful artist whose life is so vital?

Do you buy her
The gifts that she wants
Or do you just bake her
The cakes and make fonts
Filled with sparkles of light,
Or do you just look in the mirror
To placate her?

Whatever you do
Know this: It is true
That she will still be there, will
Still love you for you.

It's Just a Nudge

How do you listen
To non-words and non-language
The voice that whispers?
You tune in, you feel it flow
An instinct that pushes. Go.

Threshold Guardians

Stepping through the door
Into creativity
Warmed by morning sun.
Hold the door open
Yearning to yell No! Go: Run!
Familiar cold, please.
Wedge foot firmly in.
Make your story come to life;
Capture light in jars.
Courage takes practice.
Unravel time post-thought-lost.
Mum can do anything.
So laugh and step on,
Towards that dream filled with love
Warmed by morning sun.

Threshold Guardian II

On the brink of deep new change
A guardian will soon appear
It might not be a person form
But in an illness take a toll.
It comes when you are oh! So near
To feeling safe, success and clear
That you may find surprise unkind
And wish you had weeks' more time.
Just like the troll who guards the bridge
You're facing a surmountable ridge
For trolls are dumb and you are smart
You need only know just what to ask
Your *Inside Girl* who shakes and fears
Will drag you down if you don't hear
So ask what is the payoff wanted,
And find the key to passing.
Keep your heart in the right place
And hug that girl with frightened face
She made this guardian appear
She can make it *dis*appear!
Healing is a back-and-forth,
You'll need resilience to go forth
Recognise the guardian true
And it will never harm you.

Transition

Sometimes,
When we are on the brink
Of delivering on that new thing
We bail out
Screaming,
I'm done, I'm out, I'm leaving!
It's called transition.
And most mums know
That your creature is
About to show.
So when you feel that you are done—
Persist.
Nobody said birthing anything
Is easy.

Promises Kept

While you drape yourself
Over my leg
Snuggled into warmth, the
Smell of comfort only mum can give,
I gaze at you.
And promise to honour us
In whatever shape
I take.

Elen of the Ways

Deep in the grasslands of
Internal time
Stands a woman with antlers,
A bow on her back.
And if you ask nicely she'll
Point to the track.
Beware of your wishes,
Of what you may ask,
She'll get you back home:
Not from where you start.
Her name could be Elen,
Keeper of Ways,
She's ancient and hidden
Deep in your maze.
She answers 'most always
When woman is lost,
Giving directions
To life, but not
To your dreaming
—So ask, but
Just know that the fork in the road
Is for you,
That Elen will take you
Home to your birth.
Prepare to let go of
Things you hold close, for they
May not be yours,
You're just playing host.
The loss, it will hurt, and
Then you'll be mad
Fuelling your grief until
Acceptance is had.
When you reach your own door,
Knocking dirt from your boots,

Will you remember that woman
Whose sign show your roots
Or will you just thunder off into the sun?
This isn't a battle.
But you'll still think you've won.

Nobody Cares Because It's Just Love

There is more love in
Art than you will suppose, 'cos
Art is heart said quick.

Give In

The choice you make
When art you make
Is not to take
A righteous stake
Instead you rake
The chocolate cake
That fell, you ache
To have a taste!
So just go bake
And stand and wait
And art will take
The shape it takes,
The artist makes
But doesn't make
For forces great
Give you that, mate.

Sugar-free

Guilt is a useless
Emotion, my mum told me.
This time is yours. Enjoy.

Transition II

Sometimes a mum-to-be
Will stand up, excuse herself
And try to flee.
Transition is the hardest time;
To birth this darling—
A midwives' ironic paradigm
Is what it means:
The end draws nigh.
So, too, in creative life
The time of change nearing, rife with
Doubt and discovery;
Limitations can make one flee.
Facing down the end of things
Requires courage.
Beyond the end, darkness reigns;
This endless spiral gains and gains
Those first new steps are scary see,
You've shifted your identity.
No-one knows if it succeeds
So doubt and anxiety begin to breed,
Instead of confident creativity.
Know this, that focus on the process
Reminds us that
This
Inflection
Too
Shall
Pass.

Earth-bound

Rebels break the rules
Exchewing any structure.
Drop: Things always fall.

Rebellion is an Illusion

Yes. Thank you for asking—
Earth. Rules-bound, in simpatico.
We: Are Earth, each one,
Living, as rocks we breathe.
Ask—Can you release us from
Rules. Whose shape enables us,
Gifts. In structure we revel.
Breaking. Bonds loosen in defiance
For only in using rules
Can any perception as to breaking
Occur:
Wisely.
Carefully.
Acted,
While those who don't play
Stay stuck.

... Leap.

Realising the immensity of
Identifying newly born,
Sacred creativity upon us, we
Kiss the sky
        and leap.

For The Love of an Emerald

A great irony
Is that jealousy's bell rings
So you take action.
        She is enticing,
Garbed in the greens of healing
Twinkling eyes, saying: *Look!*
        Long-suffering souls,
Starving for meals of beauty,
Follow her, drooling.
        Believing looks feed,
Building walls against their own
Listening skills, lest
        Some day they become
The object of jealousy
And her entourage.
        Once you know she resides
In that land hidden away,
Tools that can be used
        To make her head turn,
You, too, rest on pedestals
Of greatness, knowing
        That the green shining
Beauty with bells ringing bright
Healed you; for you could
        Listen, trust, and act—
Releasing hypnotic sign;
As you watch her pass you by.

Emote

Deep the waters run;
Fast the waters flow;
Still the mind awaits;
Fear emotions show.
Be in place alone,
Find the heartwise place,
Shine your art's halo,
Feel that cold excite:
Sparks in body's bright
Led to joy in this
Place of earthly bliss.

Timeless

In the fine dusty light of
A sparkling, starlit morn
Absent of expectation and
Allowing the dawn to unfold
From birdsong to
Fires in the sky
You become, just for a moment,
The creature you were born to be.

Shoot the Rapids

The speed with which you
Lose your recognition of
Letting-go-ness is
Deafening.
   Remember it.
Control stops birth in its tracks,
Expectation aborts fulfilment.
You are a vessel,
Thrown to the winds of time and
Tossed by the seas of destiny
And you are merely
   Witness.
Yours is an experience, a
Beingness that drives the
Light into the world.
A terrific and beautiful creature
Whose only task is to
   Create.
Breathe your way over the
Rising waves of tides who
Carry you to places undreamed,
   Unseen,
And take with you your notebook.
Sketch the places you go,
Make verse from the
Magnificence of memory if you must,
   Just never let go
Of that wisdom that says
You are the water.

Always A Smoker

Casting a glance behind me
I see how far I have come.
Lifetimes lived and dug,
An archaeology project
With no shovels or brushes,
No artefacts or funding,
Just a notebook, a pen,
And a willingness to be led.
Witnessing the emergence of
The child-person whom I had
Lost to the darkened caverns of
Harsh stone-walled prison,
I see her dance beside me.
She is glorious, demanding,
And the waves of pure energy that sing
Songs that I scramble to capture
Float on a breeze that kisses only my cheek.
For each of us has weather,
And if we choose to splash
In even the tiniest puddle,
We can make music and
Paint with the richness of Earth.
Fearing the loss of your song,
Chasing quavers as they shimmer by,
The day slips,
Slides away,
And with it
I realise that recovery is endless.

Soulful Song

If my heart could whisper to yours
Without your ears getting in the way,
Without your mind casting clouds of doubt and
         sorrow for lives lost, gone, run away;
Without those stories you hold filling your hands and your
arms, leaving
         no space for you to grasp;
Without that context of life telling you that this songbook
         is filled with lies;
Then my heart would sing sweetly,
Lifting your very being
Into a realm of possibility,
Warming your belly with the gentle flame of an abiding love,
that
Tingles in rivulets under your skins now and always.
Binding us,
You and me, in a timeless web of destiny,
Calling together the mother trees who stand witness and who
         yet act in their passivity;
Calling home the knowing that in this,
This very moment
We are creating,
Are enmeshed in an
Eternal moment of artistry.
And in it
We are not alone.

Spirals of Ignorance

Who was it who said
'Your joy must become a "job"'?
Poor soul. They didn't know.

Tied by Tension

Voices raised in con-
Tradiction shine a light on
Peaceful middle way.
        You just can't see it
Because choice is a decision
And responsibility;
Creating is free,
Accept the tension you feel:
Choice is always both.

Kissed in the Dark

Woken by gentle kisses in the dark
I open my eyes to see
Your beaming, gentle smile.
This moment,
Suspended in its own existence
Is a forever bond,
That ignites all fires,
Keeps them burning.
It teaches me
Timelessness,
Patience,
Being.

Homecoming

Emerging from the dark forest path
Squinting in the light of morning,
Perpetual in its radiance and
Golden in its hue,
Any trials of grief and loss you
Scattered in the slippery gravel that
Spilled from pockets down fallen slopes and were
Cast from your person to lighten your load while climbing
Rock-faces you had no choice but to scale,
Are forgotten.
Embracing the clarity of who you truly are,
You breathe with me.
Skin to skin, warm to touch,
Calmed by the mere presence of mother
You show me that this dawn
Is destiny.
In its strong defining light
This transition,
This birth,
Brings me home.

The End

This is not the end.
No, no. This is where the story starts.
Life-long, long life art.

Don't miss out!

Visit the website below where you can sign up to receive emails whenever Leticia Mooney publishes a new book. There is no charge and no obligation. You will get no emails from Leticia other than new release notifications.

→ **https://leticiamooney.com/new-releases-list**

Other titles by Leticia Mooney

- Music Journalism 101

- The Art of Postcard Writing

- Brilliant Blawgs: A playbook for creating and maintaining strategic blogs that clients & prospects love

- The Ultimate Guide to Project Management for Creatives

- Demonic Possession is Viral: Infection of the masses (Leticia Writes spiritual books as Gabriele Francis)

- Ultimatum

- Business by the Moon: The scheduling method that grows your business and your wellness at the same time

About the Author

Leticia Mooney is an Australian author whose works grapple with notions of 'place'. Leticia works in a multiplicity of form, from essays to poetry. Her mission is to kindle a light in everyone who reads her work. Visit her official website at leticiamooney.com to discover more.

www.ingramcontent.com/pod-product-compliance
Lightning Source LLC
Chambersburg PA
CBHW030831090426
42737CB00009B/972